GET TOUGH!

HOW TO WIN
IN HAND-TO-HAND FIGHTING

AS TAUGHT TO THE BRITISH COMMANDOS
AND THE U. S. ARMED FORCES

By
MAJOR W. E. FAIRBAIRN

Illustrated by "Hary"

The Naval & Military Press Ltd

Published by

The Naval & Military Press Ltd
Unit 5 Riverside, Brambleside
Bellbrook Industrial Estate
Uckfield, East Sussex
TN22 1QQ England

Tel: +44 (0) 1825 749494

www.naval–military-press.com
www.nmarchive.com

This book is published strictly for historical purposes.
The Naval & Military Press Ltd expressly bears no responsibility or liability of any type,
to any first, second or third party, for any harm, injury, or loss whatsoever.

In reprinting in facsimile from the original, any imperfections are inevitably reproduced
and the quality may fall short of modern type and cartographic standards.

PREFACE

The method of hand-to-hand fighting described in this book is the approved standard instruction for all members of His Majesty's forces. The Commandos, and parachute troops, harrying the invasion coasts of Europe, have been thoroughly trained in its use. Britain's two-million Home Guard are daily being instructed in its simple but terrible effectiveness. The units of the United States Marine Corps who were stationed in China between 1927 and 1940 learned these methods at my own hands when I was Assistant Commissioner of the Shanghai Municipal Police.

There will be some who will be shocked by the methods advocated here. To them I say "In war you cannot afford the luxury of squeamishness. Either you kill or capture, or you will be captured or killed. We've got to be tough to win, and we've got to be ruthless—tougher and more ruthless than our enemies."

It is not the armed forces of the United Nations alone who can profit by learning how to win in hand-to-hand fighting. Every civilian, man or woman, who ever walks a deserted road at midnight, or goes in fear of his life in the dark places of a city, should acquaint himself with these methods. Once mastered, they will instil the courage and self-reliance that come with the sure knowledge that you are the master of any dangerous situation with which you may have to cope.

The methods described in this book I have carefully worked out and developed over a period of many years. They owe something to the famous Japanese judo (jiu-jutso), and something else to Chinese boxing. But, largely, they were developed from my own experience and observation of how most effectively to deal with the ruffians, thugs, bandits, and bullies of one of the toughest waterfront areas in the world.

Although every method described in the following pages is practicable—and so proved by the author and his students by years of experience, it is not essential to master them all. I suggest that at first you select about ten which, for reasons of your height, weight, build, etc., seem most suitable, and specialize in mastering these thoroughly.*

Do not consider yourself an expert until you can carry out every movement *instinctively* and *automatically*. Until then, spend at least ten minutes daily in practice with a friend. At first, practice every movement slowly and smoothly. Then gradually increase your speed until every movement can be executed with lightning rapidity.

I should like in conclusion to give a word of warning. Almost every one of these methods, applied vigorously and without restraint, will result, if not in the death, then certainly in the maiming of your opponent. Extreme caution, then, should be exercised in practice, care being taken never to give a blow with full force or a grip with maximum pressure. But, once closed with your enemy, give every ounce of effort you can muster, and victory will be yours.

CAPTAIN W. E. FAIRBAIRN

* The author will be glad to answer questions from readers concerning the execution of the methods described in this book. Address the author in care of the publisher, enclosing a self-addressed stamped envelope.

CONTENTS

		PAGE
BLOWS		1
1	Edge-of-the-Hand	2
2	Chin Jab	4
3	Boot (Side Kick)	6
3A	Boot Defense	8
3B	Boot ("Bronco Kick")	10
4	Knee	12
RELEASES		15
5	From a Wrist Hold (One Hand)	16
5A	From a Wrist Hold (Two Hands)	18
6	From a Strangle Hold (One Hand)	20
6A	From a Strangle Hold (Two Hands) . . .	22
7	From a Bear Hug (Front, Over the Arms) . . .	24
7A	From a Bear Hug (Front, Over the Arms) alternative release	26
8	From a Bear Hug (Front, Arms Free) . . .	28
9	From a Bear Hug (Back, Over the Arms) . . .	28
9A	From a Bear Hug (Back, over the Arms) alternative release	30
10	From a Bear Hug (Back, Arms Free)	30
11	From a Hair Hold (Back)	32
HOLDS		35
12	Thumb Hold	36
12	Thumb Hold (cont.)	38
13	Sentry Hold	40
13	Sentry Hold (cont.)	42
14	Japanese Strangle Hold	44
14A	Japanese Strangle Hold Applied from in Front . .	46

			PAGE
15	Handcuff Hold	. . . .	48
16	Bent-Arm Hold	. . . .	50
17	Head Hold .	. . . .	52

THROWS 55

18	Hip Throw .	. . . .	56
19	Wrist Throw	. . . .	58
20	Back Break .	. . . .	60

MISCELLANEOUS ADVICE 63

21	Chair and Knife	. . . .	64
22	The Match-Box Attack	. . . . . .	66
23	Smacking the Ears .	. . . .	68
24	The Art of Getting Up from the Ground	. . .	70
24A	Getting Up from the Ground (Backwards)	. .	72
25	Attack with a Small Stick or Cane	. . . .	74
25	Attack with a Small Stick or Cane (cont.)	. . .	76
25	Attack with a Small Stick or Cane (concl.)	. . .	78
26	Various Methods of Securing a Prisoner	. . . .	80
26	A—From the Handcuff Hold	. . . . . .	82
26	B—"The Grape Vine"	. . . .	84
26	C—The Chair	. . . .	86
26	D—A Substitute for Handcuffs	. . . . .	88
27	Break-Aways from "Come-Along" Grips	. . .	90
27	A—Your Opponent Has Hold of You as in Fig. 108	92
27	B—Your Opponent Has Hold of You as in Fig. 109	92

USE OF THE KNIFE 95

28	Use of the Knife	. . . .	96
28	Use of the Knife (cont.)	. . . . . .	98
28	Use of the Knife (concl.)	. . . . . .	100

		PAGE
THE SMATCHET		103
29	The Smatchet (Carrying, Drawing, and Holding) .	104
29	The Smatchet (Close-in Blows)	106
29	The Smatchet (Attacking Blows)	108

DISARMING AN OPPONENT OF HIS PISTOL . . . 111

30	Disarming an Opponent of His Pistol	112
30	A—Disarming from in Front	112
30	B—Disarming from in Front (Alternative Method)	114
30	C—Disarming from Behind	116
30	D—Disarming from Behind (Alternative Method)	118
30	E—Disarming a Third Party	120

BLOWS

NO. 1—EDGE-OF-THE-HAND

Deliver edge-of-the-hand blows with the inner (i.e., little-finger) edge of the hand, fingers straight and close together, thumb extended; contact is made with the edge only, about half-way between the knuckle of the little finger and the wrist, as shown in Fig. 1.

1. Deliver the blow with a bent arm (never with a straight arm), using a chopping action from the elbow, with the weight of the body behind it. Practise by striking the open palm of your left hand, as in Fig. 2.
2. There are two ways in which this blow can be delivered:
   (a) *Downwards*, with either hand;
   (b) *Across*, with either hand; the blow always being delivered outwards, with the palm of the hand downwards, never on top (Fig. 3).
3. Attack the following points on your opponent's body, delivering every blow as quickly as possible:
   (a) The sides or back of the wrist;
   (b) The forearm, half-way between the wrist and elbow;
   (c) The biceps;
   (d) The sides or back of the neck;
   (e) Just below the "Adam's apple";
   (f) The kidneys or base of the spine.

Note.—If your opponent catches hold of you, strike his wrist or forearm; a fracture will most likely result. This would be almost impossible with a blow from a clenched fist.

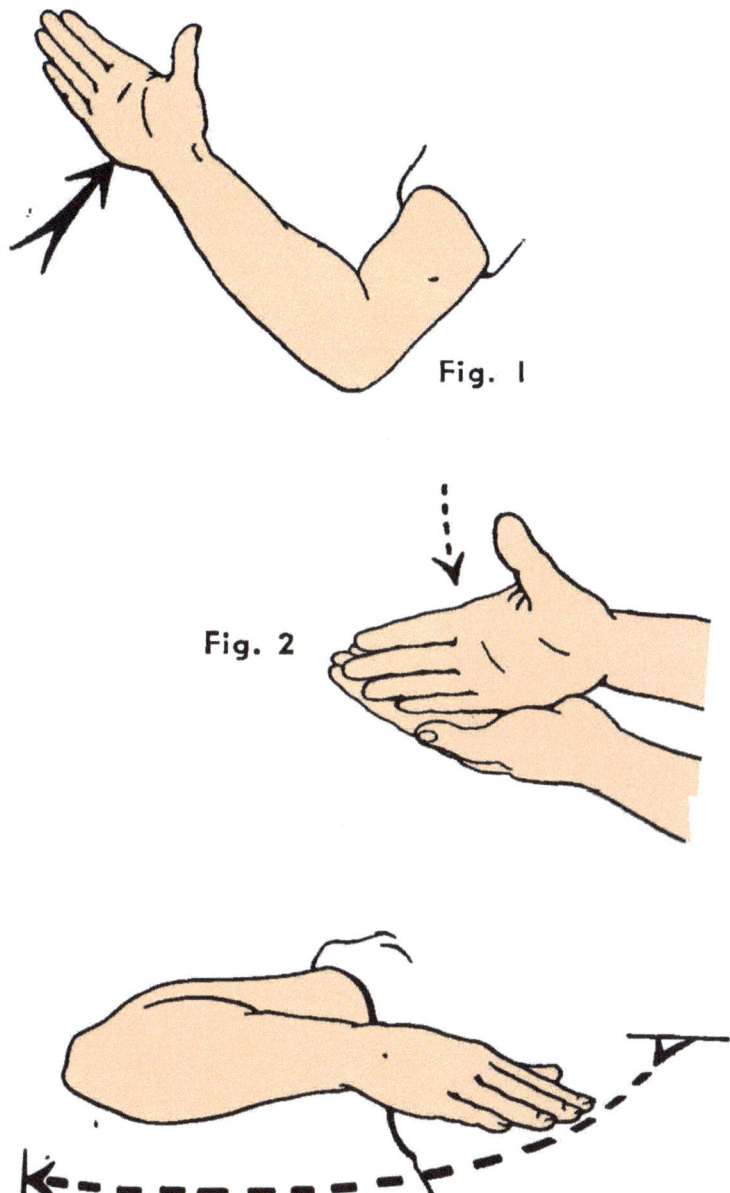

Fig. 1

Fig. 2

Fig. 3

NO. 2—CHIN JAB

Deliver this blow with the heel of your hand, full force, with the weight of your body behind it, and fingers spread so as to reach your opponent's eyes, as in Fig. 4. Always aim at the point of your opponent's chin (Fig. 5).

1. Deliver the blow upwards from a bent arm and only when close to your opponent. The distance the blow will have to travel will depend on the height of your opponent, but will seldom exceed six inches.
2. Never draw your hand back, thus signaling your intention of striking. From start to finish, make every movement as quickly as possible.
3. Remember that an attack, or an attempt to attack, with the knee at your opponent's testicles will always bring his chin forward and down.

Note.—Practise this blow as follows: Hold your left hand at the height of your own chin, palm downwards; jab up quickly with your right, striking your left hand, as in Fig. 6.

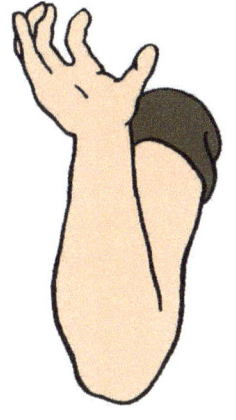

Fig. 4

Fig. 5

Fig. 6

NO. 3—BOOT (SIDE KICK)

With a few exceptions, you should always kick sideways, for you are thus able to put more force behind your blow and can, if necessary, reach farther.

1. Turn your right side to your opponent, putting the weight of your body on your left foot. Bending your left leg slightly from your knee, raise your right foot two to four inches off the ground, as in Fig. 7. Shoot your right foot outwards and upwards to your right, aiming to strike your opponent's leg just below the knee-cap.
2. Follow the blow through, scraping down your opponent's shin with the edge of your boot from the knee to the instep, finishing up with all your weight on your right foot, smashing the small bones of his foot. If necessary, follow up with a chin jab with your left hand (Fig. 8).

Note.—Where the kick is to be made with the left foot, reverse the above.

Fig. 7

Fig. 8

NO. 3A—BOOT DEFENSE

Your opponent has seized you around the body from in front, pinning your arms to your sides.

1. Having put your weight on one foot, raise the other and scrape your opponent's shin-bone downwards from about half way from the knee, finishing up with a smashing blow on his foot (Fig. 9).
2. An alternative method to Fig. 9, permitting you to use the inner edge of the boot, is shown in Fig. 10.

Note A.—Whether you should use the outside or inside of your boot will depend upon how the weight of your body is distributed at the time. Provided that you are equally balanced on both feet, you can use either; otherwise, use the one opposite to that on which you have your weight.

Note B.—If seized from behind, stamp on your opponent's foot with the heel of either boot, turning quickly and following up with a chin jab with either hand.

Fig. 9

Fig. 10

NO. 3B—BOOT ("BRONCO KICK")

Your opponent is lying on the ground.

1. Take a flying jump at your opponent, drawing your feet up by bending your knees, at the same time keeping your feet close together (Fig. 11).
2. When your feet are approximately eight inches above your opponent's body, shoot your legs out straight, driving both of your boots into his body, and smash him.

Note.—It is almost impossible for your opponent to parry a kick made in this manner, and, in addition, it immediately puts him on the defensive, leaving him only the alternative of rolling away from you in an attempt to escape. Further, although he may attempt to protect his body with his arms, the weight of your body (say 150 pounds), plus the impetus of your flying jump (say another 150 pounds), will drive your heels into your opponent's body with such terrific force that you will almost certainly kill him. Steel heel-plates on your boots will make his attack even more effective.

Practise this kick on a dummy figure or on the grass as in Fig. 12.

Fig. 11

Fig. 12

NO. 4—KNEE

This blow can be delivered only when you are very close to your opponent.

1. Putting the weight of your body on one leg, bend the knee of the other by drawing your heel slightly backwards, and drive your knee quickly upwards into your opponent's testicles (Fig. 13).

Note.—This blow is frequently used to bring your opponent into a more favorable position for applying the chin jab (Fig. 14).

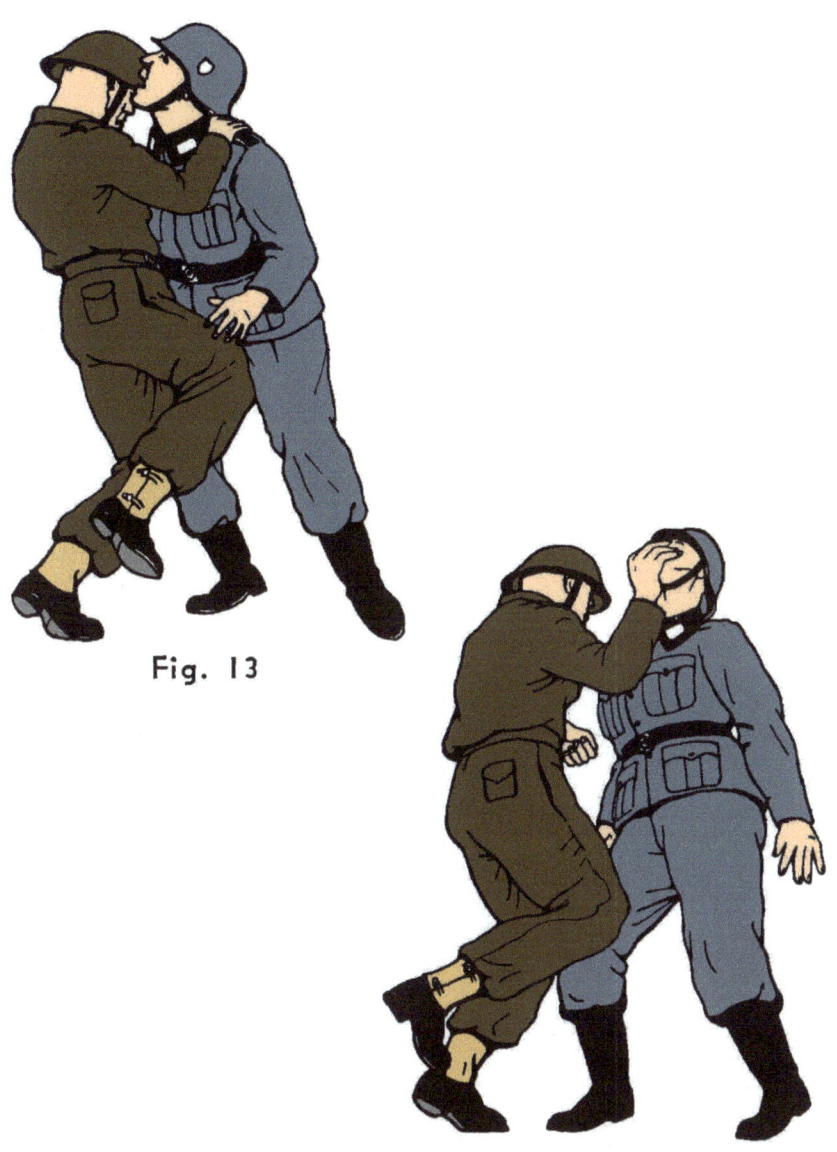

Fig. 13

Fig. 14

RELEASES

NO. 5—FROM A WRIST HOLD (ONE HAND)

1. You are seized by the right wrist, as in Fig. 15. Bend your wrist and arm towards your body, twisting your wrist outwards against your opponent's thumb (Fig. 16).

Note A.—This must be accomplished with one rapid and continuous motion.

Note B.—No matter with which hand your opponent seizes either of your wrists, *the important thing to remember is to twist your wrist against his thumb.*

Fig. 15

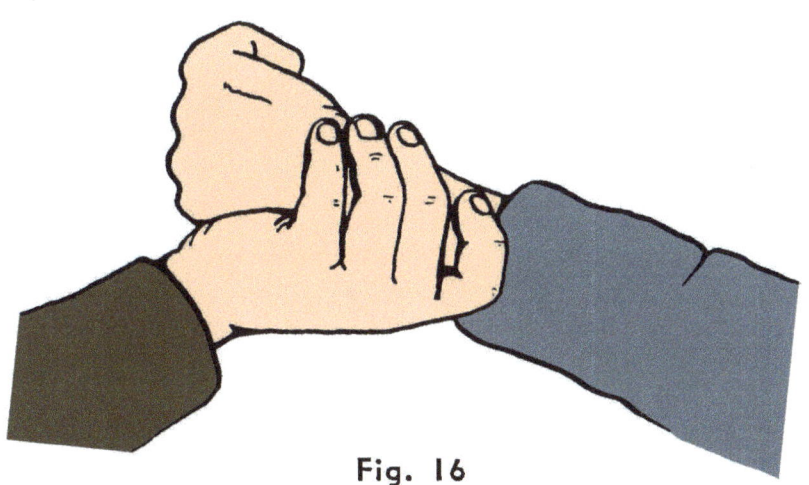

Fig. 16

NO. 5A—FROM A WRIST HOLD (TWO HANDS)

1. You are seized by the left wrist, by two hands, as in Fig. 17, your opponent's thumbs being on top. Reach over and catch hold of your hand with your right. Pull your left hand sharply towards your body, against his thumbs (Fig. 18).

Note A.—The pressure on his thumbs, which is slightly upwards and then downwards, will force him to release his hold immediately.

Note B.—Follow up with chin jab, edge-of-the-hand, or knee kick to the testicles.

Should your opponent seize you as in Fig. 19 (his thumbs underneath), pass your right hand under and catch hold of your left hand as in Fig. 20. Pull down sharply towards you.

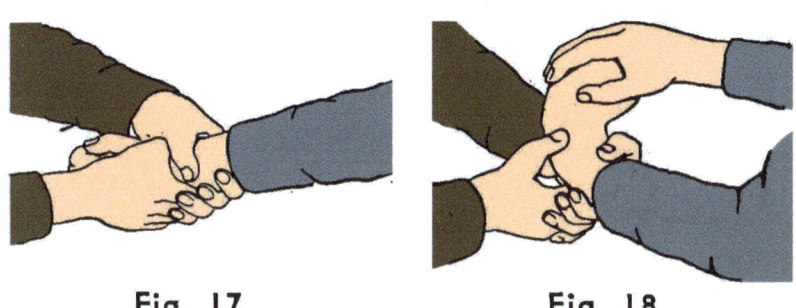

Fig. 17   Fig. 18

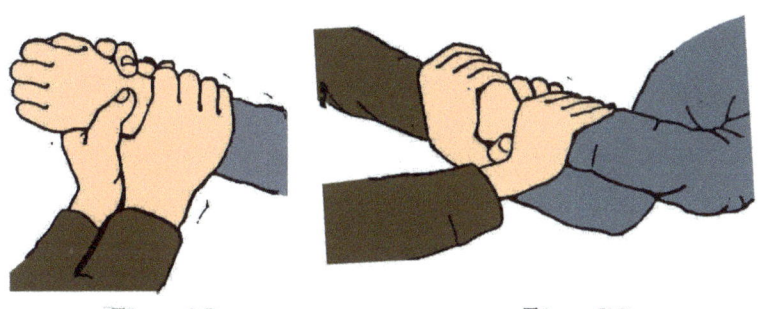

Fig. 19   Fig. 20

NO. 6—FROM A STRANGLE HOLD (ONE HAND)

You are seized by the throat, as in Fig. 21, and forced back against a wall.

1. With a smashing blow with the edge of your right hand, strike your opponent's right wrist towards your left-hand side. Follow up with a knee kick to his testicles (Fig. 22).

Fig. 21

Fig. 22

NO. 6A—FROM A STRANGLE HOLD (TWO HANDS)

You are seized from in front by the throat, as in Fig. 23.

1. With your left hand seize your opponent's right elbow from underneath, your thumb to the right.
2. With your right hand, reach over his arms and seize his right wrist (Fig. 24).
3. With your right arm apply pressure downwards on his left arm; at the same time, with a circular upward motion of your left hand, force his elbow towards your right side. This will break his hold of your throat and put him off balance (Fig. 25).
4. Keeping a firm grip with both hands, turn rapidly towards your right-hand side by bringing your right leg to your right rear. Follow up with edge-of-the-hand blow on his right elbow (Fig. 26).

Note.—All the above movements must be one rapid and continuous motion.

Fig. 23

Fig. 24

Fig. 25

Fig. 26

NO. 7—FROM A BEAR HUG (FRONT, OVER THE ARMS)

You are gripped around the waist (Fig. 27).

1. Knee your opponent in the testicles.
2. With the outer or inner edge of either boot, scrape his shin-bone from about half way from the knee and follow through by stamping on his instep.
3. If, as a soldier, you are wearing a helmet, smash him in the face with it.
4. Seize his testicles with either hand.

Fig. 27

NO. 7A—FROM A BEAR HUG (FRONT, OVER THE ARMS) Alternative Release

You are gripped around the waist (Fig. 27).

1. If possible, bite his ear. Even though not successful, the attempt will cause him to bend forward and into a position from which you can seize his testicles with your right hand (Fig. 28).
2. Reach over his arm with your left forearm (Fig. 29).
3. Apply pressure on his right arm with your left (causing him to break his hold), and force his head downwards. Smash him in the face with your right knee (Fig. 30).

If necessary, follow up with edge-of-the-hand blow on back of his neck.

Note.—Should your opponent anticipate your intention when you are in the position shown in Fig. 29 and resist the pressure of your left arm (¶ 3), go after his eyes with your left hand as in Fig. 30A, and follow up with a knee to the testicles.

Fig. 28

Fig. 29

Fig. 30

Fig. 30A

NO. 8—FROM A BEAR HUG (FRONT, ARMS FREE)

You are gripped around the waist (Fig. 31).

1. Place your left hand in the small of his back and apply a chin jab, as in Fig. 32.

If necessary, knee him in the testicles.

NO. 9—FROM A BEAR HUG (BACK, OVER THE ARMS)

You are gripped around the chest (Fig. 33).

1. If you are wearing a helmet, smash your opponent in the face with it.
2. Stamp on his feet with either foot.
3. Seize him by the testicles with your right or left hand.

Fig. 31

Fig. 32

Fig. 33

NO. 9A—FROM A BEAR HUG (BACK, OVER THE ARMS) Alternative Release

You are gripped around the chest (Fig. 33).

1. Seize your opponent's testicles with your left hand (causing him to break his hold).
2. Pass your right arm over his right (Fig. 34).
3. Slip out from under his arm by turning to your left and stepping backwards with your right foot, seizing his right wrist with both hands and jerking it downwards. Finish up by kicking him in the face (Fig. 35).

NO. 10—FROM A BEAR HUG (BACK, ARMS FREE)

You are gripped around the chest (Fig. 36).

1. If you are wearing a helmet, smash your opponent's face with it.
2. Stamp on his feet with either foot.
3. Seize his little finger with your right hand, bend it backwards, and walk out of the hold (Fig. 37).

Fig. 34

Fig. 35

Fig. 36

Fig. 37

NO. 11—FROM A HAIR HOLD (BACK)

You are seized by the hair from behind and pulled back, as in Fig. 38.

1. With both hands, seize your opponent's right wrist and arm with a very firm grip, making him keep the hold shown in Fig. 39.
2. Turn to your left (inwards, towards your opponent) by pivoting on your left foot. This will twist his arm.
3. Step backwards as far as possible with your right foot, jerking his hand off your head in a downward and backward direction between your legs (Fig. 40).

Note.—It is possible that this will tear quite a bit of your hair out by the roots, but it is very unlikely that you will notice it at the time.

4. Keep a firm grip on his wrist and arm, and follow up with a smashing kick to your opponent's face with the toe of your right boot.

Note A.—All the above movements must be one rapid and continuous motion.

Note B.—When in the position shown in Fig. 40, you can increase the force of your kick to the face by pulling your opponent's arm slightly upwards and towards you. This movement also enables you to get back on balance.

Fig. 38 Fig. 39

Fig. 40

HOLDS

NO. 12—THUMB HOLD

This is the most effective hold known, and very little exertion on your part (three to four pounds' pressure) is required to make even the most powerful prisoner obey you. It is possible also for you to conduct him, even if resisting, as far as he is able to walk. You have such complete control of him that you can, if necessary, use him as cover against attack from others.

The movements you have to make to secure this hold are very complicated, which is mainly the reason why it is almost unknown outside of the Far East. But the advantage one gains in knowing that he can effectively apply this hold more than repays for the time that must be spent in mastering it.

First concentrate on making every move slowly, gradually speeding up until all movements become one continuous motion. When you have thoroughly mastered the hold, then learn to secure it from any position in which you have secured your opponent.

It should be understood that this hold is not a method of attack, but simply a "mastering hold," which is applied only after you have partially disabled or brought your opponent to a submissive frame of mind by one of the "follow up" methods (BLOWS).

Should your opponent not be wearing a helmet or similar protection which covers his ears, the following will be found to be a very simple method of making him submissive:

Cup your hands and strike your opponent simultaneously over both ears (Fig. 41). This will probably burst one or both ear drums and at least give him a mild form of concussion. It can be applied from the front or from behind.

Fig. 41

NO. 12—THUMB HOLD (cont.)

Stand facing your opponent and slightly to his left.

1. Insert your right thumb between the thumb and forefinger of his left hand, your fingers under the palm of his hand, your thumb to the right (Fig. 42).
2. Seize his left elbow with your left hand, knuckles to the right, and thumb outside and close to your own forefingers (Fig. 43).
3. Step in towards your opponent; at the same time, turn your body so that you are facing in the same direction, simultaneously forcing his left forearm up across his chest and towards his left shoulder by pulling his elbow with your left hand over your right forearm and forcing upwards with your right hand (Fig. 44).

Release the hold with your left hand just as soon as you have pulled his elbow over your right forearm, and hold your opponent's left elbow very close to your body.

4. Keeping a firm grip on the upper part of his left arm with your right arm, immediately seize the fingers of his left hand with your left. This will prevent him from trying to seize one of the fingers of your right hand and also give you an extra leverage for applying pressure as follows:
5. Press down on the back of his hand towards your left-hand side with your right hand. Should your opponent be a very powerful man and try to resist, a little extra pressure applied by pulling his fingers downwards towards your left-hand side with your left hand will be sufficient to bring him up on his toes and convince him that he has met his master (Fig. 45).

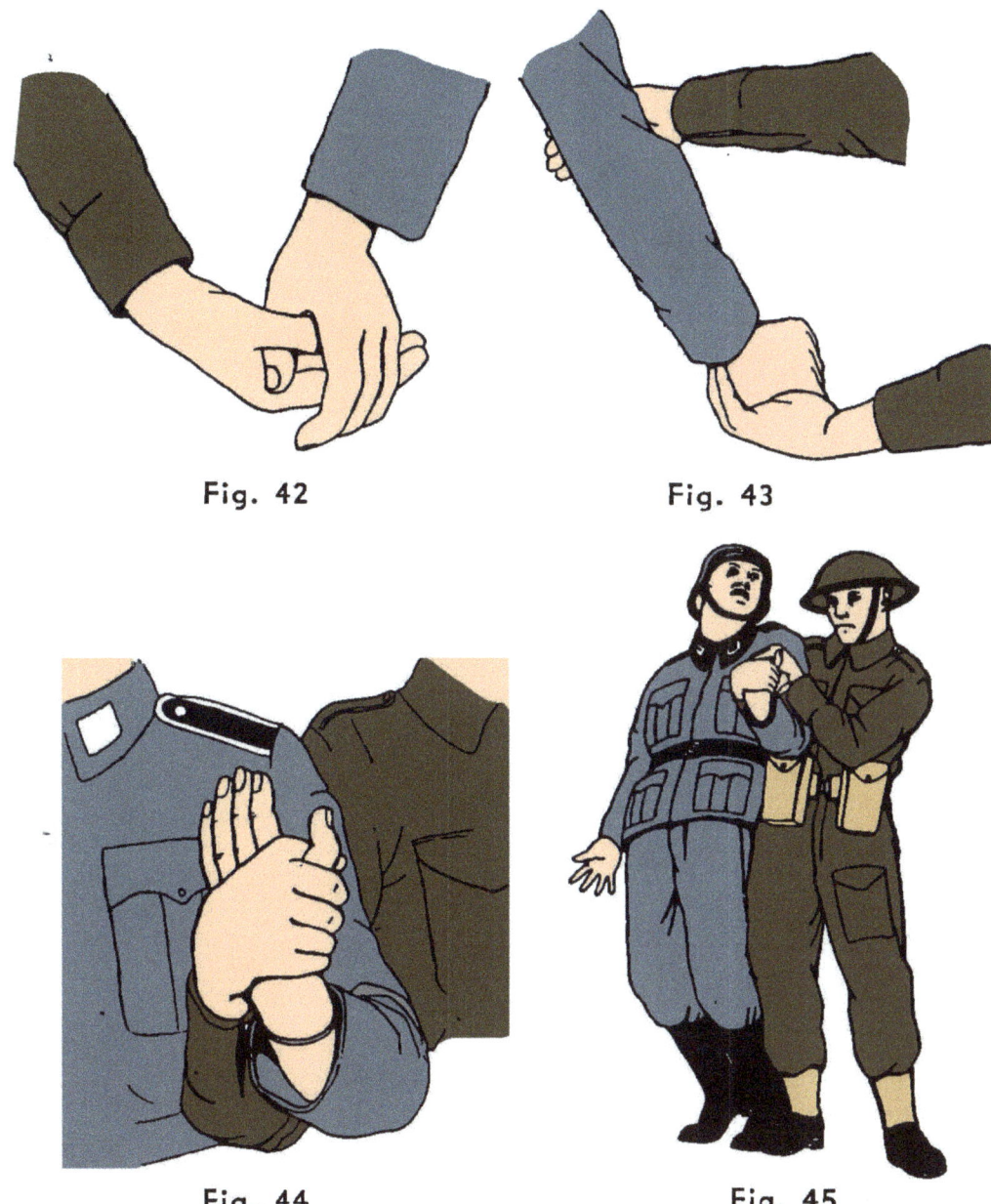

Fig. 42

Fig. 43

Fig. 44

Fig. 45

NO. 13—SENTRY HOLD

The successful execution of this method of attack on a sentry—presupposing thorough mastery of every move—depends entirely on careful preparation. First, the man selected to make the attack should be an *expert at stalking*. The stalk or approach should be made during the hours of dark or semi-dark, and the sentry should be kept under observation long enough for the attacker to familiarize himself with the sentry's movements and equipment.

Now let us assume that conditions are somewhat as follows:

1. The sentry's rifle is slung or carried on his right shoulder.
2. He is wearing a steel helmet covering the back of his neck and his ears.
3. He is wearing a respirator on the small of his back, projecting as much as six inches (see Fig. 46).
4. There are other sentries within shouting distance.

These conditions are not too favorable for the attacker, but are what might have to be met, and training should be carried out under conditions as near as possible to those which would be met in actual war.

Note.—The stalker should not be handicapped with any equipment, other than a knife or a pistol. He should wear rubber or cloth shoes, socks pulled well up over the trousers, cap-comforter well pulled down, with the collar of his blouse turned up and his hands and face camouflaged (See Fig. 47, page 43).

Fig. 46

NO. 13—SENTRY HOLD (cont.)

1. Approach the sentry from behind to within three to four feet and take up the position shown in Fig. 47. This will permit you to make a lightning-like attack by springing on him.
2. With the fingers and thumb of your left hand fully extended, *strike* him across the throat with the inner edge of your left forearm (i.e. with the forearm bone), and simultaneously *punch* him with your clenched right hand in the small of his back or on his respirator case (Fig. 48).

The effect of these blows, if applied as above, will render your opponent unconscious or semi-conscious. Further, the blow on the throat will cause your opponent to draw in his breath, making it impossible for him to shout and give the alarm.

3. The blows should be immediately followed with a very fast movement of your right hand from the small of his back, over his right shoulder, clapping it over his mouth and nose (Fig. 49). This will prevent him from breathing or making a noise if the blow on the throat was not effectively applied.

Very likely the blows on his throat and in the small of his back will cause him to drop his rifle or will knock his helmet off his head. Should this happen, do not attempt to prevent their falling on the ground. Just keep still for about ten seconds, after which it is unlikely that anyone having heard the noise will come to investigate. Retaining your hold around his neck with your left arm, drag him away backwards.

Note.—The extraordinary effectiveness of this hold will be readily understood if you have a friend apply it on you as above, being careful to exert no more than one-twentieth of the required force.

Fig. 47

Fig. 48

Fig. 49

NO. 14—JAPANESE STRANGLE HOLD

1. Approach your opponent from behind.
2. Place your left arm around his neck, with your forearm bone bearing on his "Adam's apple."
3. Place the back of your right arm (above the elbow) on his right shoulder and clasp your right biceps with your left hand.
4. Place your right hand on the back of his head.
5. Pull him backwards with your left forearm and press his head forward with your right hand, and strangle him (Fig. 50).

Note.—Should your opponent attempt to seize you by the testicles:

(*a*) Keep your grip with both arms, straightening out the fingers and thumbs of both hands. With the edge of your left hand in the bend of your right arm, place the edge of your right hand just below the base of the skull.

(*b*) Step back quickly, at the same time jolting his head forward with the edge of your right hand, and dislocate his neck (Fig. 51).

(*c*) If your opponent is a taller man than yourself, making it difficult for you to reach his right shoulder with your right arm, as in Fig. 50, bend him backwards by applying pressure on his neck with your left arm. If necessary, punch him in the small of the back, as shown in Fig. 48, page 43, and bring him down to your own height.

Fig. 50

Fig. 51

NO. 14A—JAPANESE STRANGLE HOLD APPLIED FROM IN FRONT

1. Stand facing your opponent.
2. Seize his right shoulder with your left hand and his left shoulder with your right hand.
3. Simultaneously push with your left hand (retaining the hold) and pull towards you with your right hand, turning your opponent around (Fig. 52). Your left arm will now be around his neck and most likely you will have caused your opponent to cross his legs, making it almost impossible for him to defend himself.
4. Place the back of your right arm (above the elbow) on his right shoulder and clasp your right biceps with your left hand.
5. Grasp the back of his head with your right hand, and apply pressure by pulling him backwards with your left forearm and pressing his head forward with your right arm (Fig. 52A).

Note.—Although the final position and the method of applying pressure are identical with that shown in No. 14 on the previous page, there is a difference in the amount of pressure necessary to strangle your opponent. If his legs are crossed (and they almost always will be when he is suddenly twisted round in this manner), approximately only half the amount of pressure will be required.

Fig. 52   Fig. 52A

NO. 15—HANDCUFF HOLD

1. You are facing your opponent. Make a dive at his right wrist, seizing it with both hands, right above left, and jerk it violently downwards, as in Fig. 53. This will produce a considerable shock, amounting almost to a knockout blow on the left side of his head.
2. Swing his arm up to the height of your shoulder, at the same time twisting his arm towards you so as to force him off-balance on to his left leg (Fig. 54).
3. Keeping his arm at the height of your shoulder, pass quickly underneath it by taking a pace forward with your right foot. (It may be necessary for you to reduce your height to permit your doing this; do so by bending your legs at the knees.) Turn inwards towards your opponent, jerking his arm downwards, as in Fig. 55.
4. Step to his back with your left foot, and, with a circular upward motion, force his wrist well up his back. Retain the grip with your left hand and seize his right elbow with your right hand, forcing it well up his back. Then slide your left hand around his wrist, bringing your thumb inside and finger over the back of the hand, and bend his wrist. Apply pressure with both hands until your opponent's right shoulder points to the ground (Fig. 56).

Note A.—This is a very useful hold for marching your prisoner a short distance only. For a longer march, a change to the Thumb Hold (Fig. 45, page 39) is recommended.

Note B.—A method of tying up your prisoner is shown on page 83 (Figs. 98 and 99).

Fig. 53

Fig. 54

Fig. 55

Fig. 56

NO. 16—BENT-ARM HOLD

Note.—Students are strongly recommended to specialize in mastering this hold.

1. Your opponent has taken up a boxing stance, or raised his right arm as if about to deliver a blow.
2. Seize his right wrist with your left hand, bending his arm at the elbow, towards him (Fig. 57). Continue the pressure on his wrist until his arm is in the position shown in Fig. 58.

Note.—These movements must be one rapid and continuous motion. Note that forcing your opponent's right forearm backwards places him off-balance, making it almost impossible for him to attack you with his left fist.

3. Immediately step in with your right foot, placing your right leg and hip close in to your opponent's thigh.
4. Pass your right arm under the upper part of his right arm, seizing his right wrist with your right hand above your left.
5. Keeping a firm grip with both hands, force his right elbow and arm against your chest, applying pressure by jerking his wrist towards the ground. At the same time, force the forearm bone of your right arm up and in to the back muscles of the upper part of his right arm (Fig. 59).
6. Should your opponent, when in this position, attempt to strike you with his left hand: Straighten out the fingers and thumb of your right hand, placing the edge of the hand over your left wrist, and apply pressure by a sudden jerk upwards of your right forearm, taking care to keep his elbow well in to your chest (Fig. 60).

Fig. 57

Fig. 58

Fig. 59

Fig. 60

NO. 17—HEAD HOLD

Approach your opponent from the front.

1. Keeping the fingers of your right hand straight and thumb extended, strike him on the left side of his neck with the inside of your right forearm (Fig. 61). This blow will render your opponent "punch-drunk" or dazed.
2. Immediately after delivering the blow with your right forearm, slide it around your opponent's neck, simultaneously stepping across his front with your right leg, bending him forward from the waist and catching hold of your right wrist with your left hand (Fig. 62).
3. Force your right forearm bone into the right side of his face (anywhere between the temple and the chin will do) by pulling on your right wrist with your left hand and forcing downwards on the left side of his face with your body.

Note.—Observe that the outside of your right forearm is resting on your right thigh and that the weight of your body is being forced on to your right leg by pressure from your left foot. Any attempt of your opponent to seize your testicles should immediately be countered by a slight increase of pressure. If necessary, apply an edge-of-the-hand blow as follows: Release your hold with your left hand, straighten up slightly, and apply the blow on the left side of his neck.

Fig. 61

Fig. 62

THROWS

NO. 18—HIP THROW

You are facing your opponent.

1. Seize his equipment, arms, or clothing slightly above the height of his elbows. Pull down with your right hand and lift up with your left hand, pulling him off-balance. Simultaneously shoot your left leg as far as possible behind him, keeping your left leg rigid and close up to his thigh. Take care that your left foot is pointing as in Fig. 63.
2. Continue the downward pull of your right hand and the upward lift of your left hand, at the same time bending forward and downwards from your waist towards your right foot. All the above movements must be one rapid and continuous motion and will throw your opponent as in Fig. 64. Follow-up with a kick on his spine with either boot, somewhere near the small of his back.

Note.—An alternative method of applying the Throw when dealing with an opponent approaching you on your left side is as follows:

1. Seize his equipment or left arm with your right hand and pull downwards, simultaneously striking him up under the chin with your left hand (Chin Jab) and kicking his legs from under him with a backward kick of your rigid left leg, as in Fig. 65. This will throw your opponent backwards with smashing force, after which it will be a simple matter for you to dispose of him in any manner you may wish.

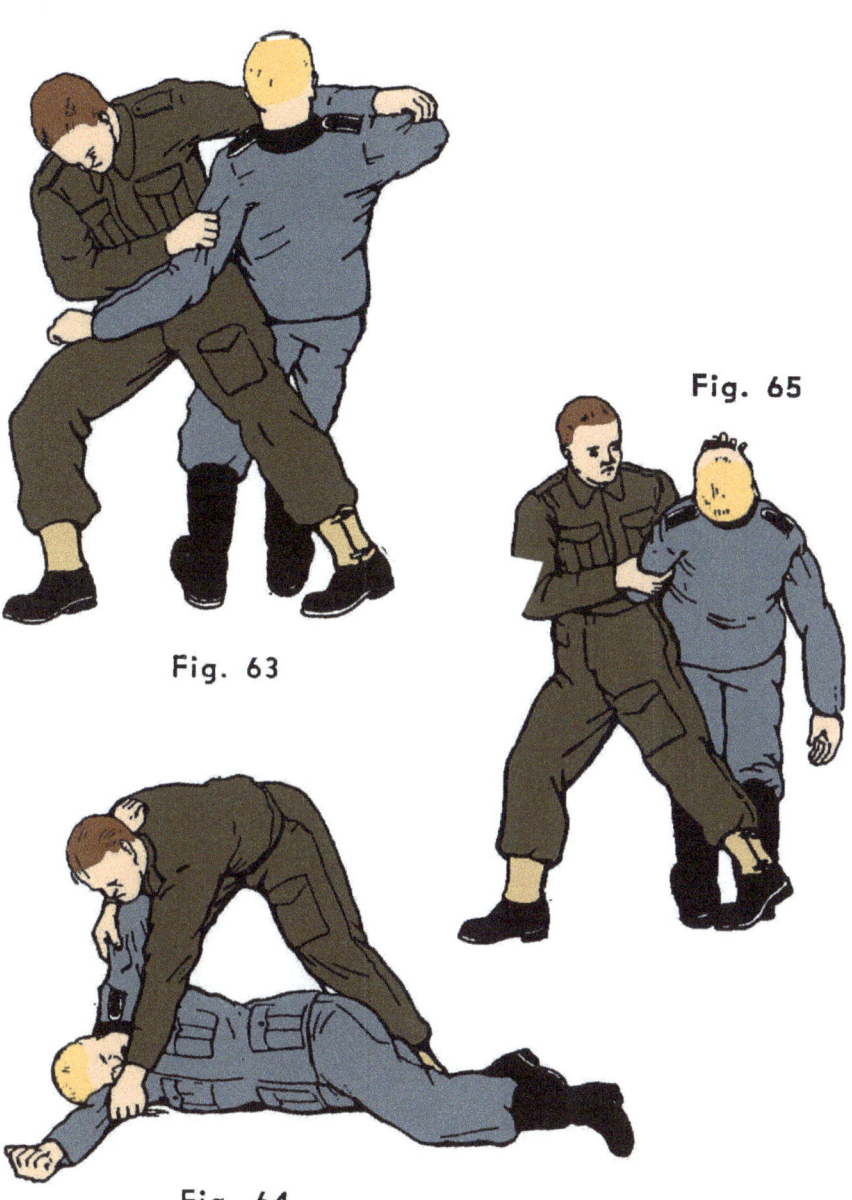

Fig. 63

Fig. 65

Fig. 64

NO. 19—WRIST THROW

Because of the unusual manner in which your opponent's hand is seized at the initial start of this throw, you should first learn the hold as follows:

1. Force your left thumb into the back of your opponent's right hand, between the small bones of his first and middle fingers, your fingers passing around to the palm of his hand.
2. Force your right thumb into the back of this same hand, between the small bones of his middle and third fingers, your fingers passing around to the palm of his hand.
3. Bend his hand towards him by pressure of your thumbs on the back of his hand and backward pressure on the palm and wrist with your fingers (Fig. 66).
4. Retain your hold with your left hand, take your right away, and permit his right arm to hang naturally at his side. (Remember, this is only practice.) You will then be in the position shown in Fig. 67. (Back of your left hand towards your right-hand side, your fingers around his thumb towards the palm of his hand, your thumb forced in between the small bones of his first and second fingers.)
5. Bend his arm, by a circular upward motion, towards your left-hand side, turning the palm of his hand towards him; then force both your thumbs into the back of his hand (Fig. 66).
6. Applying pressure on the back of his hand and on his wrist (as in ¶ 3), force his hand towards the ground on your left-hand side. This will throw him on to his right-hand side. To finish your opponent off, jerk up on his right arm, simultaneously smashing down on his lower ribs with your right boot (Fig. 68).

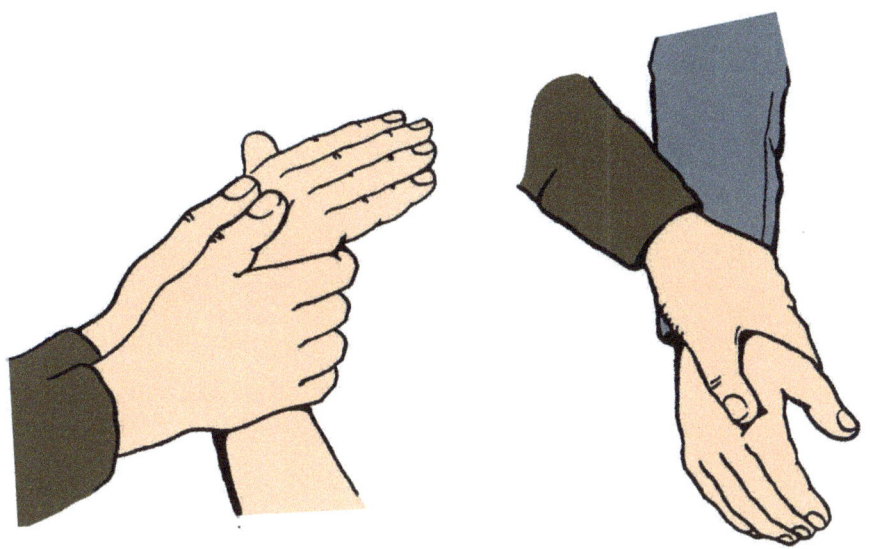

Fig. 66   Fig. 67

Fig. 68

NO. 20—BACK BREAK

1. Approach your opponent from his left-hand side, bend your legs slightly, reach down, and seize him by passing your right arm over his chest and your left arm under his legs, just behind the knee, as in Fig. 69.
2. Lift him up, mainly by straightening your legs, as in weight lifting, to approximately the height of your chest, as in Fig. 70.
3. Take a short pace forward with your right foot, bending your right leg so that the upper part (thigh) is approximately parallel to the ground. With all the strength of your arms, assisted by the forward movement of the upper part of your body, smash him down on your right knee and break his spine (Fig. 71).

Note.—If you carry out these directions correctly, you will be surprised how easily you can lift a man much heavier than yourself. You are partially aided by the fact that your opponent will instinctively try to save himself by clutching hold of you with one or both hands. Provided that you use the weight of your body in your downward smash, he cannot prevent you from breaking his spine.

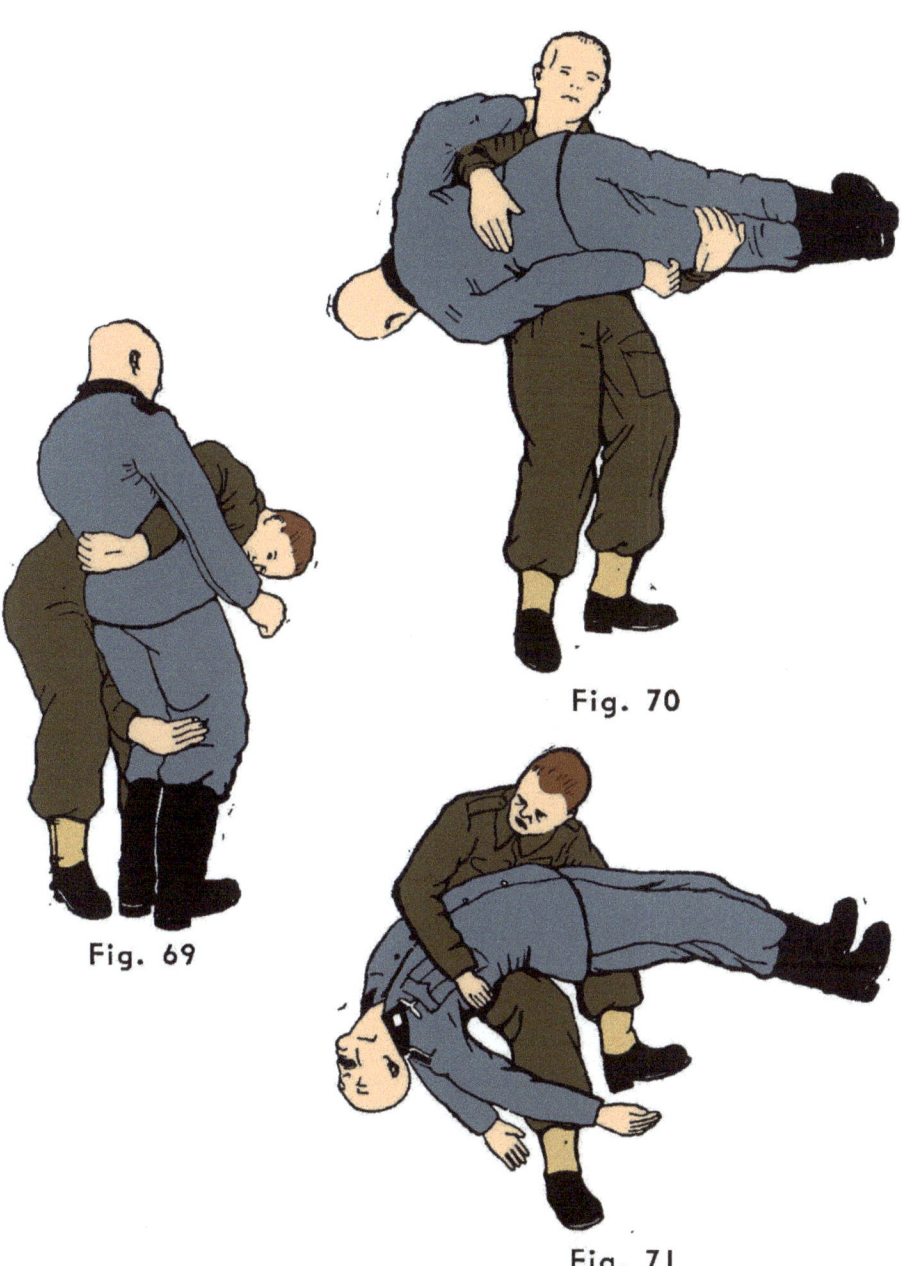

Fig. 69

Fig. 70

Fig. 71

MISCELLANEOUS ADVICE

NO. 21—CHAIR AND KNIFE

Most lion tamers consider a small chair to be sufficient to keep a lion from attacking them. Should you be so fortunate as to have a chair handy when your opponent is attacking you with a knife, seize the chair as in Fig. 72. Rush at him, jabbing one or more of the legs of the chair into his body. The odds in favor of your overpowering your opponent are roughly three to one, and well worth taking (Fig. 73).

Fig. 72

Fig. 73

NO. 22—THE MATCH-BOX ATTACK

You are sitting down, say, in a railway coach. Your opponent, who is on your left, sticks a gun in your ribs, holding it in his right hand.

1. Take a match-box and hold it as in Fig. 74, the top of the box being slightly below the finger and thumb.
2. Keeping the upper part of the right arm close to the right side of your body, with a circular upward motion of your right fist, turning your body from the hip, strike your opponent hard on the left side of his face, as near to the jawbone as possible (Fig. 75); parry the gun away from your body with your left forearm.

Note.—The odds of knocking your opponent unconscious by this method are at least two to one. The fact that this can be accomplished with a match-box is not well-known, and for this reason is not likely to raise your opponent's suspicion of your movements. Naturally, all movements, from the start of the blow, must be carried out with the utmost speed.

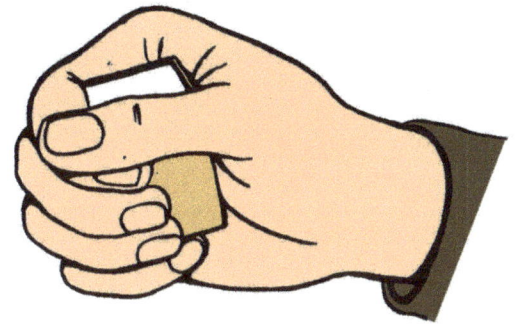

Fig. 74

Fig. 75

NO. 23—SMACKING THE EARS

This method should be applied when your opponent has no protection over his ears.

1. Cup your hands, keeping the fingers and thumbs bent and close together, as in Fig. 76.
2. Strike your opponent simultaneously over both ears, using five to ten pounds force (Fig. 77).

Note.—This will probably burst one or both ear-drums, give him at least a mild form of concussion, and make him what is known in boxing circles as "punch-drunk." You will then have no difficulty in dealing with him in any way you wish.

So that you may realize what the effect of a blow given as above is like, apply it on yourself, as in Fig. 77A. Care must be taken to use *only* half a pound force with each hand.

Fig. 76

Fig. 77

Fig. 77A

NO. 24—THE ART OF GETTING UP FROM THE GROUND

You will have noted that no holds or locks on the ground are demonstrated. The reason for this is:

(*a*) *THIS IS WAR:* your object is to kill or dispose of your opponent as quickly as possible and go to the assistance of your comrades.

(*b*) Once on the ground, you are more vulnerable to attack. (See No. 3B, Bronco Kick.)

(*c*) It takes months of constant daily practice to master the art of falling, and personal instruction from a qualified instructor is essential.

(*d*) There is a vast difference between falling on mats in a gymnasium and falling on a road or rocky ground. Even a roll on to a stone or a small stump of a tree, should it press into the kidneys, would certainly put you out of the fight permanently.

It is, therefore, obvious that you should concentrate on remaining on your feet. No attempt is made to teach you how to fall, but the following guides are given on how to get back on your feet if you do fall or are thrown:

1. You are on the ground, as in Fig. 78.
2. Turn your body sharply towards your left-hand side, stomach to the ground, rising by the help of the right forearm and right knee to the position shown in Fig. 79.
3. Pushing on the ground with both hands, force yourself backwards into the position shown in Fig. 80, and then stand up.

Note.—All the above movements must be one rapid and continuous roll or twist of the body.

If, when in the position shown in Fig. 80, your opponent is behind you, place your right foot as near as possible to your left hand (Fig. 81), turn sharply on both feet towards your left-hand side, and you will find yourself facing your opponent.

Fig. 78

Fig. 79

Fig. 80

Fig. 81

NO. 24A—GETTING UP FROM THE GROUND (BACKWARDS)

1. You have fallen on to your back on the ground.
2. Lie flat on your back and place your right arm at an angle of 90 degrees from the body, the back of your hand on the ground and your head turned towards your left shoulder (Fig. 82).
3. Raise your legs from the waist and shoot them over your right shoulder (Fig. 83). When in this position, allow your right arm and hand to turn with your body.
4. Bend your right leg and bring it to the ground as close to your right arm as possible. Keeping your left leg straight reach as far back with it as possible (Fig. 84).
5. Your left hand will be on the ground approximately opposite your right knee. Press on the ground with both hands and force yourself up on to your right knee. Continue the pressure until you are on your feet (Fig. 85).

Note.—The reason for keeping your feet apart in the movement shown in ¶ 4 is that you will immediately be on-balance when you come up on your feet. This is a very important point to note and is very seldom taken care of by the average man. A man off-balance can be pushed down again with a few pounds' pressure of either hand. Moreover, he cannot administer an effective blow or even defend himself properly.

Fig. 82

Fig. 83

Fig. 84

Fig. 85

NO. 25—ATTACK WITH A SMALL STICK OR CANE

A man without a weapon to defend himself, especially after long exposure, is very likely to give up in despair. It is remarkable what a difference it would make in his morale if he had a small stick or cane in his hand. Now, add to this the knowledge that he could, with ease, kill any opponent with a stick, and you will then see how easy it is to cultivate the offensive spirit which is so essential in present-day warfare.

1. A small stick of 18 to 24 inches in length and about 1 inch in thickness will make an ideal weapon. (If one is not available, it can be broken off a tree.)

Note.—If you are to be successful in the application of this method, it is essential for you to have the element of surprise on your side. This can best be obtained by taking the position shown in Fig. 86.

2. Retaining your hold of the stick with your right hand, swing the other end up and catch it in your left hand about six inches from the end. This should be done without looking down at your hands or stick. Pay particular attention to the position of the hands (Fig. 87).

Note.—The reason for using this unusual hold of the stick should be obvious. It is not at all likely that anyone (not previously aware of this particular method of attack) would have the slightest suspicion that he was in danger of being attacked.

Fig. 86

Fig. 87

NO. 25—ATTACK WITH A SMALL STICK OR CANE (cont.)

You are close up and facing your opponent, as in Fig. 88.

1. Strike your opponent *across* the stomach with the left end of the stick by a vicious circular motion towards your right-hand side.

    In delivering this blow, there are four essential points that must be carried out simultaneously:

    (*a*) Your loose grip on the stick, both hands (Fig. 87), must be changed to one as strong as possible.

    (*b*) The movement of your left hand is towards your right-hand side.

    (*c*) The movement of your right hand is inwards to the left, but much shorter than that of the left hand, because of your right hand's coming against your right side.

    (*d*) The movement of your left foot is forward towards the right. This permits you to put the weight of your body behind the blow. See Fig. 89.

Note.—This blow *across* your opponent's stomach would not, if he were wearing thick clothing, put him out, but it would surely make him bring his chin forward, which is exactly the position you want him in.

2. Keeping the firmest possible grip of the stick with both hands, jab upwards with the end of the stick (left-hand end) and drive it into his neck and kill him (Fig. 90). The mark you are after is the soft spot about two inches back from the point of the chin.

Fig. 88

Fig. 89

Fig. 90

NO. 25—ATTACK WITH A SMALL STICK OR CANE (concl.)

You have missed your opponent's chin when you attacked as in Fig. 90.

    3. Smash him down the face with the end of the stick, as in Fig. 91, putting all the weight of your body behind the blow.

    4. If necessary, follow-up with a smash across the left side of your opponent's face with the right-hand end of the stick, as in Fig. 92.

Note.—You have taken a step to your left front with your right foot to permit of the weight of the body being behind the blow.

    5. If at any time after the initial attack across the stomach your opponent's head is high in the air, exposing the front part of his neck: Aim to strike the "Adam's apple" with the center of the stick, putting every ounce of strength behind the blow. This should kill him, or at least knock him unconscious (Fig. 93).

Note.—Methods No. 2 (the point, up under the chin) and No. 5 (the center, into the "Adam's apple") are finishing-off or killing blows, but you must first bring your opponent into the position that permits you to deal them effectively. Method No. 1 (the point across the stomach) will, on account of its unexpectedness, enable you to accomplish this, and your attack should always start with the stomach attack.

Fig. 91

Fig. 92

Fig. 93

NO. 26—VARIOUS METHODS OF SECURING A PRISONER

All raiding parties should have among their equipment a small roll of adhesive tape, preferably of one or more inches in width, and a length of silk rope or cord, about a quarter of an inch in diameter and about five yards in length, for gagging and securing a prisoner whom they wish to leave unguarded.

To Gag a Prisoner.—Force a piece of cloth or a lump of turf into his mouth; then place two or more strips of adhesive tape, approximately four and a half inches in length, firmly over his mouth, taking care not to cover his nostrils.

Tying the Highwayman's Hitch.—This knot should be practised on a pole or the back of a chair, until it can be done in the dark.

1. Holding the cord with a *short* end (about two feet), pass it behind the pole, with the *short* end to the left and the *long* to the right (Fig. 94).
2. Pass the *long* end, in a loop, up and over the pole and through the loop held in the left hand. Then pull down on the *short* end with the right hand (Fig. 95).
3. Pass the *short* end of the cord, in a loop, up and over the pole and through the loop held in the left hand, and form the knot shown in Fig. 96.
4. Holding the loop in the left hand, pull down on the *long* end of the cord, pass the left hand through the loop and then pull on both *ends* of the cord (Fig. 97).

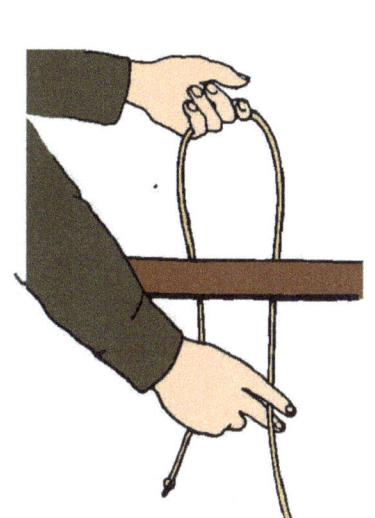

Fig. 94

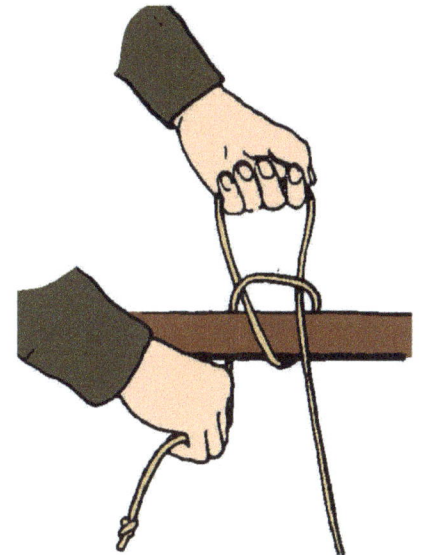

Fig. 95

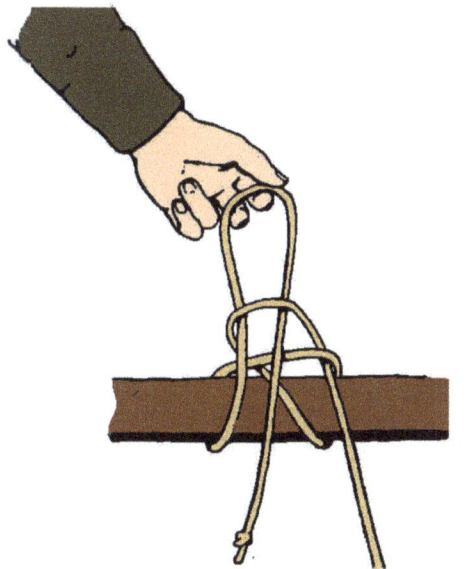

Fig. 96

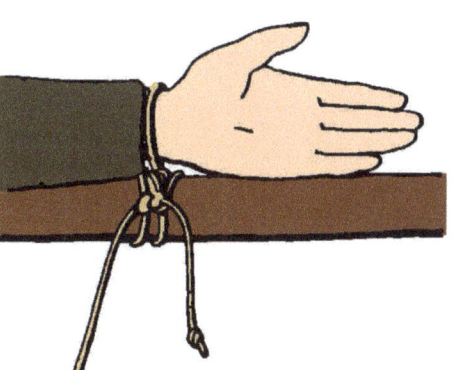

Fig. 97

NO. 26—VARIOUS METHODS OF SECURING A PRISONER (cont.)

A—From the Handcuff Hold

1. Throw your prisoner to the ground on his stomach, tying his wrists together behind his back by means of the Highwayman's Hitch, as in Fig. 98, and force his arms well up his back.
2. Pass the cord around his neck; then back and around his wrists again; then bend his legs backwards and tie his legs together, as in Fig. 99.

Note.—If your prisoner keeps still, he will not hurt himself, but should he attempt to struggle, he will most likely strangle himself.

Fig. 98

Fig. 99

NO. 26—VARIOUS METHODS OF SECURING A PRISONER (cont.)

B—"The Grape Vine"

Select a tree, post, or lamp-post of about seven inches in diameter.

1. Make your prisoner climb on the tree as in Fig. 100.
2. Place his right leg around the front of the tree, with his foot to the left. Place his left leg over his right ankle, as in Fig. 101, and take his left foot back behind the tree.
3. Force him well down the pole until the weight of his body locks his left foot around the tree, as in Fig. 102.

Note.—Even though you have left your prisoner's hands free, it will, if he has been forced well down the tree, be almost impossible for him to escape. Normally, the average man placed in this position would get cramp in one or both legs within ten to fifteen minutes, when it is not at all unlikely that he would throw himself backwards. This would kill him.

Caution.—To release your prisoner: Two persons are necessary, one on either side. Take hold of his legs and lift him up the tree; then unlock his legs.

Fig. 100 Fig. 101 Fig. 102

NO. 26.—VARIOUS METHODS OF SECURING A PRISONER (cont.)

C—The Chair

A chair with an open back is preferable.

1. Force your prisoner to sit on the chair, pass one of his arms through the back and the other arm around it, and tie his wrists together by means of the Highwayman's Hitch (Fig. 103).
2. Tie the upper part of his arms to the chair, one on either side (Fig. 104).
3. Tie both feet to the chair—one on either side—with only the toes of his boots resting on the ground, as in Fig. 105.
4. Gag him, if necessary.

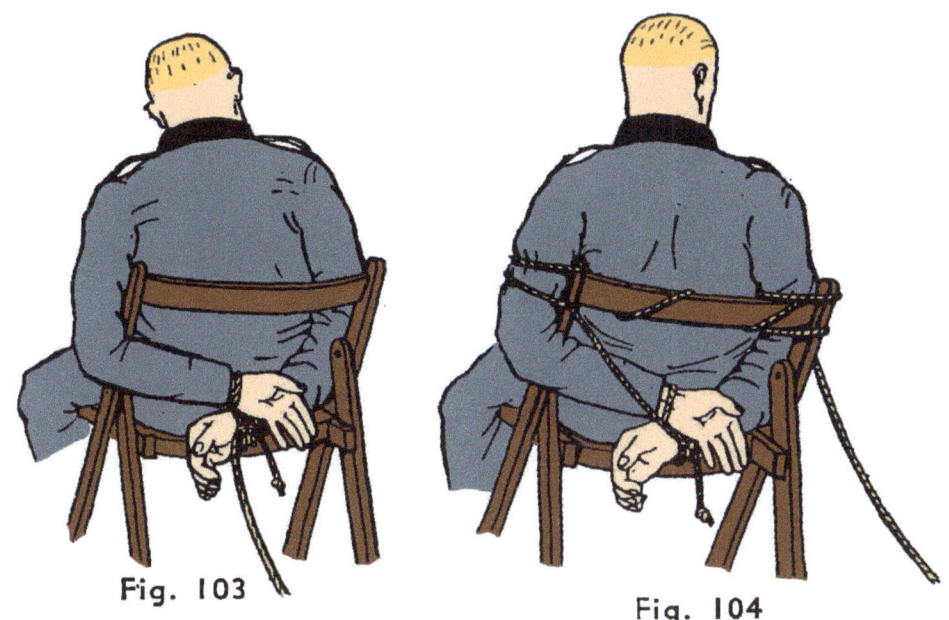

Fig. 103 Fig. 104

Fig. 105

NO. 26—VARIOUS METHODS OF SECURING A PRISONER (cont.)

D—A Substitute for Handcuffs

The following method, whereby one man can effectively control two to six prisoners, may be found very useful. A police baton, night stick, or hunting crop, preferably fitted with a cord thong, as in Fig. 106, is all that is required.

1. Cut your prisoners' trouser-belts and/or suspenders, then thoroughly search them for concealed weapons.
2. Make them all put their right wrists through the loop of the thong, and twist the baton until the thong cuts well into their wrists (Fig. 107). Then march them off.

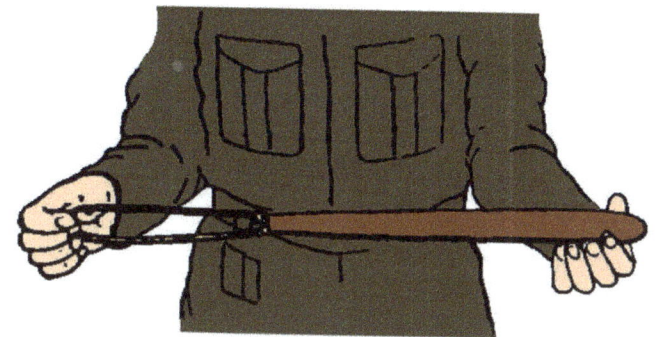

Fig. 106

Fig. 107

NO. 27—BREAK-AWAYS FROM "COME-ALONG" GRIPS

A number of so called "come-along" grips are frequently demonstrated and taught as being 100 per cent perfect, and impossible, once secured, for any man to escape. Under certain circumstances it would, indeed, be difficult and painful to escape them; also it might result in a badly strained ligament. Nevertheless, any man of average build and strength can, with at least a 50 per cent chance of success, not only break away from these holds, but he will also be in a position from which he can with ease break his opponent's limbs and, if necessary, kill him.

Two fairly well-known holds that are so regarded are shown on the opposite page: Fig. 108—Police Come-Along Grip, and Fig. 109—Collar and Wrist Hold.

You must face the fact that a man fighting for his life or to prevent capture is a vastly different person from one you may meet in competition. It is an established fact that a man in fear of death will be prepared to undertake the lifting of five times the weight he would in normal times, also that he can, under such circumstances, take about five times the usual amount of punishment.

This is not said with the idea of preparing you to take a lot of punishment should you attempt to break either of these holds, but simply to show you that even if you fail, you will not be in a much worse position than you were originally.

The question will be asked: "Why is it that these holds have been so commonly accepted as being unbreakable?" The answer is: Those of us who have made a study of the art of attack and defense well know that the average student is too inclined to demonstrate his prowess on his friends after only a few lessons, and before he has mastered even the initial movements. This often results in broken bones, etc. Further, the counter-measures used to break holds such as these are drastic in the extreme, and are shown to students only after they have proved beyond doubt that they would not wilfully mis-apply them.

Fig. 108

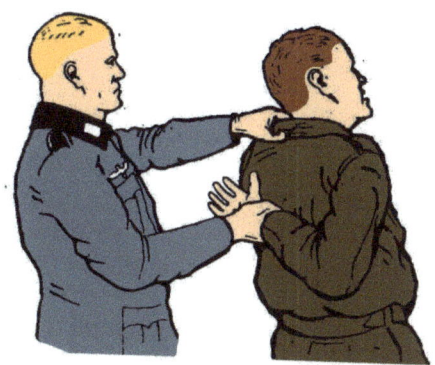

Fig. 109

NO. 27—BREAK-AWAYS FROM "COME-ALONG" GRIPS (cont.)

Note.—It is presumed that your opponent is not acquainted with the counter-methods you intend to apply.

A—Your Opponent Has Hold of You as in Fig. 108

1. Exaggerate the pain you are receiving by shouting or groaning. Try to be out of step with him, which makes it easier to apply your counter. Only resist sufficiently to prevent him from being suspicious.
2. Do not be in a hurry to apply your counter. The opening will be there every time he puts the weight of his body on his left foot.
3. Smartly jab the outside of your right leg against the outside of his left leg, forcing his leg inwards, and break it (Fig. 110), simultaneously pulling your right arm towards you, which, in addition to increasing the force of your leg blow, also permits you to bend your arm and break his hold. If necessary, apply the edge-of-the-hand blow on the back of his neck with your left hand, and kill him.

B—Your Opponent Has Hold of You as in Fig. 109

1. As in the previous method, wait until your opponent is off his guard and only resist slightly.
2. Turn sharply around towards your left-hand side, simultaneously bending your legs at the knees and your head forward to permit your head to go under his left arm. Then straighten up your head. (These movements, in addition to twisting his arm, will lock his left hand in the back of your collar.) Strike the elbow of his left arm a vicious upward jab with the palm of your right hand, as in Fig. 111. If necessary, follow up with a chin jab with your left hand, or knee to the testicles with either knee.

Fig. 108

Fig. 110

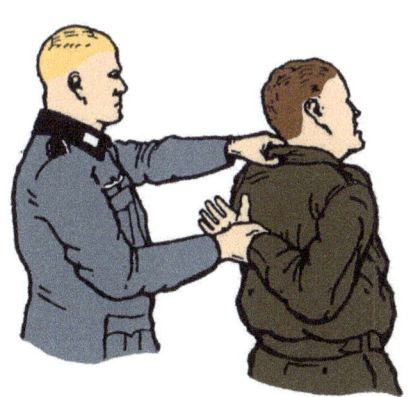

Fig. 109

Fig. 111

USE OF THE KNIFE

NO. 28—USE OF THE KNIFE

In close-quarters fighting there is no more deadly weapon than the knife. An entirely unarmed man has no certain defense against it, and, further, merely the sudden flashing of a knife is frequently enough to strike fear into your opponent, causing him to lose confidence and surrender.

In choosing a knife there are two important factors to bear in mind: balance and keenness. The hilt should fit easily in your hand, and the blade should not be so heavy that it tends to drag the hilt from your fingers in a loose grip. It is essential that the blade have a sharp stabbing point and good cutting edges, because an artery *torn* through (as against a clean cut) tends to contract and stop the bleeding. If a main artery is cleanly severed, the wounded man will quickly lose consciousness and die.

The Fairbairn-Sykes Fighting Knife (shown on the opposite page) developed by the author and a colleague, is highly recommended as possessing the requisite qualities. This knife and similar types have found wide favor among experts.

There are many positions in which the knife can be carried. Selection of this position depends upon individual preference based on length of arm, thickness of body, etc. The following considerations, however, should always be borne in mind. A quick draw (an essential in knife fighting) can not be accomplished unless the sheath is firmly secured to the clothing or equipment. Moreover, speed on the draw can be accomplished only by constant daily practice. The author favors a concealed position, using the left hand, for in close-quarters fighting, the element of surprise is the chief ingredient of success.

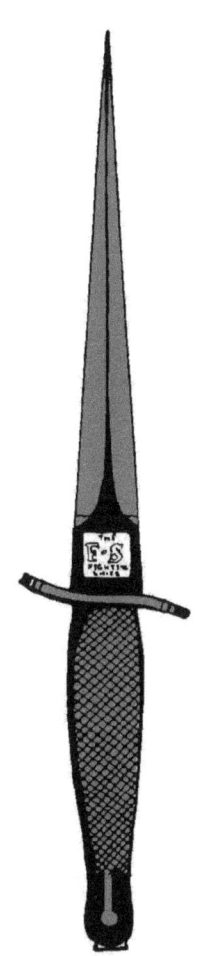

NO. 28—USE OF THE KNIFE (cont.)

Certain arteries are more vulnerable to attack than others, because of their being nearer the surface of the skin, or not being protected by clothing or equipment. Don't bother about their names so long as you can remember where they are situated.

In the accompanying diagram (Fig. 112), the approximate positions of the arteries are given. They vary in size from the thickness of one's thumb to that of an ordinary pencil. Naturally, the speed at which loss of consciousness or death takes place will depend upon the size of the artery cut.

The heart or stomach, when not protected by equipment, should be attacked. The psychological effect of even a slight wound in the stomach is such that it is likely to throw your opponent into confusion.

Explanation of Fig. 112

No.	Name of Artery	Size	Depth below Surface in inches	Loss of Consciousness in seconds	Death	
1....	Brachial	Medium	½	14	1½	Min.
2....	Radial	Small	¼	30	2	"
3....	Carotid	Large	1½	5	12	Sec.
4....	Subclavian	Large	2½	2	3½	"
5....	(Heart)	——	3½	Instantaneous	3	"
6....	(Stomach)	——	5	Depending on depth of cut		

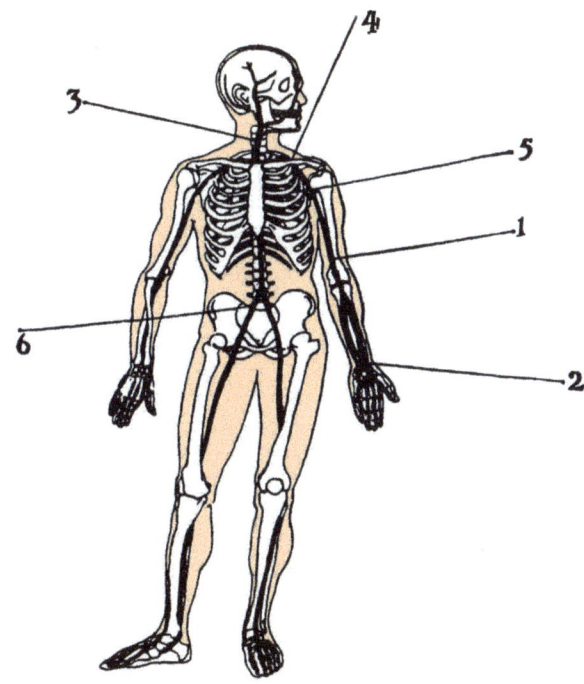

Fig. 112

NO. 28—USE OF THE KNIFE (concl.)

Method of Making the Cut

Artery #1. Knife in the right hand, attack opponent's left arm with a slashing cut outwards, as in Fig. A.

Artery #2. Knife in the right hand, attack opponent's left wrist, cutting downwards and inwards, as in Fig. B.

Artery #3. Knife in right hand, edges parallel to ground, seize opponent around the neck from behind with your left arm, pulling his head to the left. Thrust point well in; then cut sideways. See Fig. C.

Artery #4. Hold knife as in Fig. D; thrust point well in downwards; then cut.

Note.—This is not an easy artery to cut with a knife, but, once cut, your opponent will drop, and no tourniquet or any help of man can save him.

Heart #5. Thrust well in with the point, taking care when attacking from behind not to go too high or you will strike the shoulder blade.

Stomach #6. Thrust well in with the point and cut in any direction.

Note.—If knife is in left hand, when attacking arteries #1 and #2, reverse the above and attack opponent's right arm.

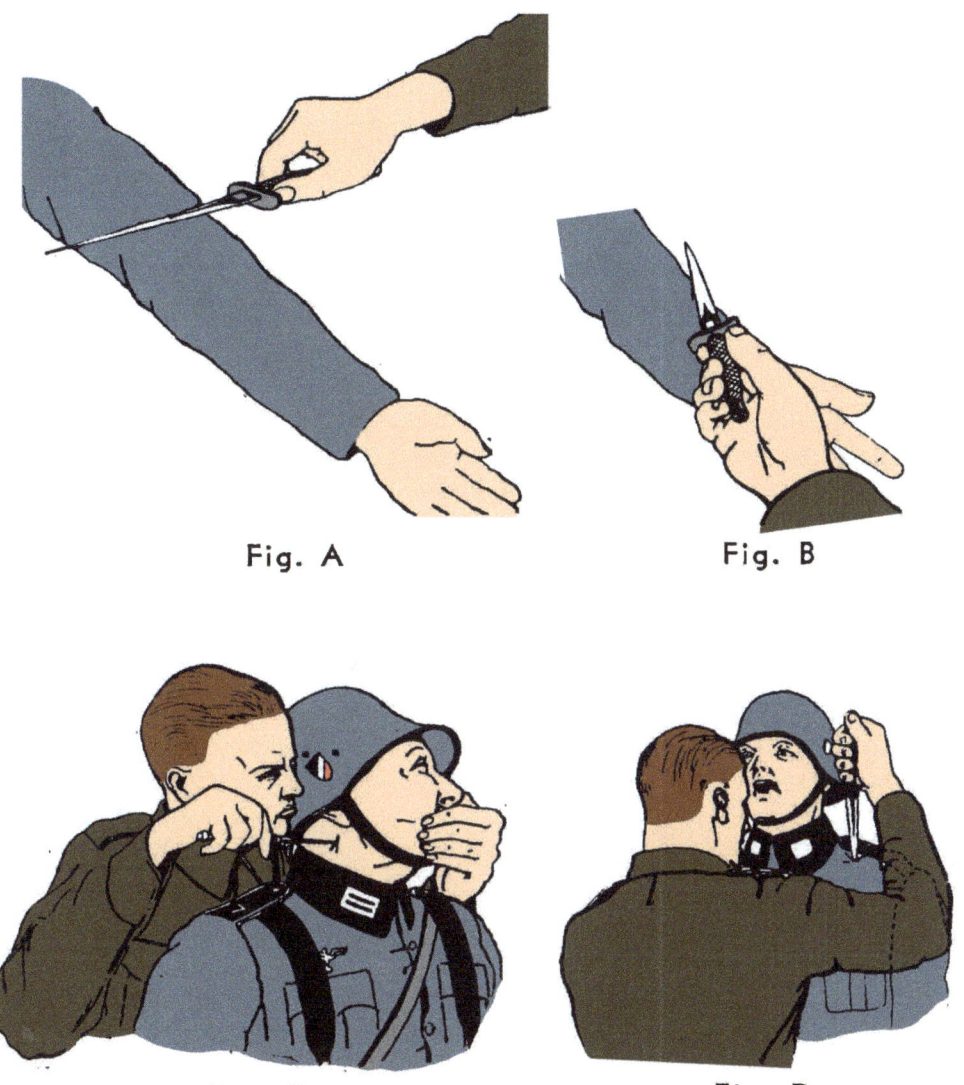

Fig. A

Fig. B

Fig. C

Fig. D

THE SMATCHET

NO. 29—THE SMATCHET

The psychological reaction of any man, when he first takes the smatchet in his hand, is full justification for its recommendation as a fighting weapon. He will immediately register all the essential qualities of a good soldier—confidence, determination, and aggressiveness.

Its balance, weight, and killing power, with the point, edge, or pommel, combined with the extremely simple training necessary to become efficient in its use, make it the ideal personal weapon for all those not armed with a rifle and bayonet.

Note.—The smatchet is now in wide use throughout the British armed forces. It is hoped that it will soon be adopted by the United States Army.

Carrying, Drawing, and Holding

1. The smatchet should be carried in the scabbard on the left side of the belt, as in Fig. 113. This permits one to run, climb, sit, or lie down.

Note.—Any equipment at present carried in this position should be removed to another place.

2. Pass the right hand through the thong and draw upwards with a bent arm (Fig. 114).
3. Grip the handle as near the guard as possible, cutting edge downwards (Fig. 115).

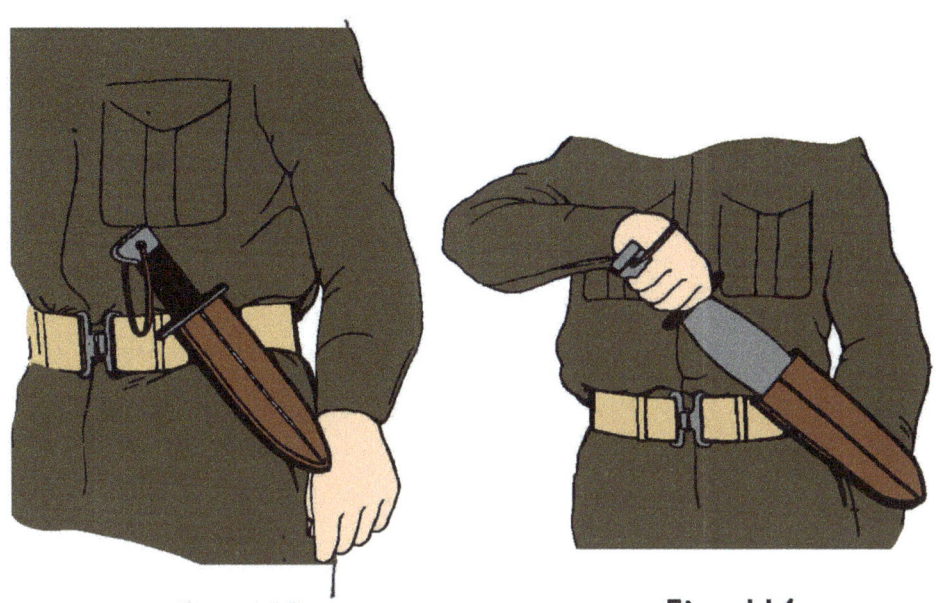

Fig. 113   Fig. 114

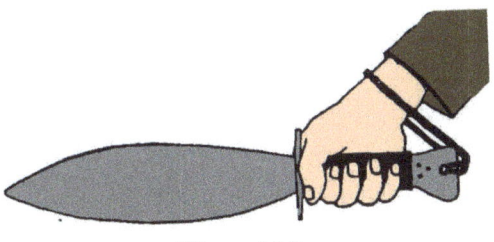

Fig. 115

NO. 29—THE SMATCHET (cont.)

Close-In Blows

1. Drive well into the stomach (Fig. 116).
2. "Sabre Cut" to right-low of neck (Fig. 117).
3. Cut to left-low of neck (Fig. 118).
4. Smash up with pommel, under chin (Fig. 119).

Fig. 116

Fig. 117

Fig. 118

Fig. 119

NO. 29—THE SMATCHET (cont.)

Close-In Blows (cont.)
5. Smash down with pommel into the face (Fig. 120).

Attacking Blows
1. "Sabre Cut" to left or right wrist (Fig. 121).
2. "Sabre Cut" to left or right arm (Fig. 122).

Fig. 120

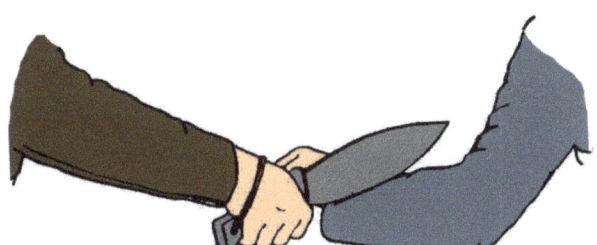

Fig. 121

Fig. 122

DISARMING AN OPPONENT OF HIS PISTOL

NO. 30—DISARMING AN OPPONENT OF HIS PISTOL

You are held up with a pistol and ordered to put your hands up. The fact that you have not been shot on sight clearly shows that your opponent wants to take you as a prisoner or is afraid to fire, knowing that it will raise an alarm.

Lead him to suppose, by your actions, manner, etc., that you are scared to death, and wait until he is close up to you. Provided that all your movements are carried out with speed, it is possible for you to disarm him, with at least a ten to one chance of success.

A—Disarming from in Front

1. Hold your hands and arms as in Fig. 123.
2. With a swinging downward blow of your right hand, seize your opponent's right wrist, simultaneously turning your body sideways towards the left. This will knock the pistol clear of your body (Fig. 124). Note that the thumb of your right hand is on top.
3. Seize the pistol with the left hand as in Fig. 125.
4. Keeping a firm grip with the right hand on his wrist, force the pistol backwards with your left hand, and knee him or kick him in the testicles (Fig. 126).

Note.—All the above movements must be one rapid and continuous motion.

Fig. 123   Fig. 124

Fig. 125   Fig. 126

NO. 30—DISARMING AN OPPONENT OF HIS PISTOL (cont.)

B—Disarming from in Front (Alternative Method)

It will be noted that in this method the initial attack is made with the left hand instead of the right as was demonstrated in the previous method.

1. Hold your hands and arms as in Fig. 127.
2. With a swinging downward blow of your left hand, thumb on top, seize your opponent's right wrist, simultaneously turning your body sideways, towards your right. This will knock the pistol clear of your body (Fig. 128).
3. Seize the pistol with the right hand, as in Fig. 129.
4. Keeping a firm grip with your left hand on his wrist, bend his wrist and pistol backwards; at the same time, knee him in the testicles (Fig. 130).

Fig. 127   Fig. 128

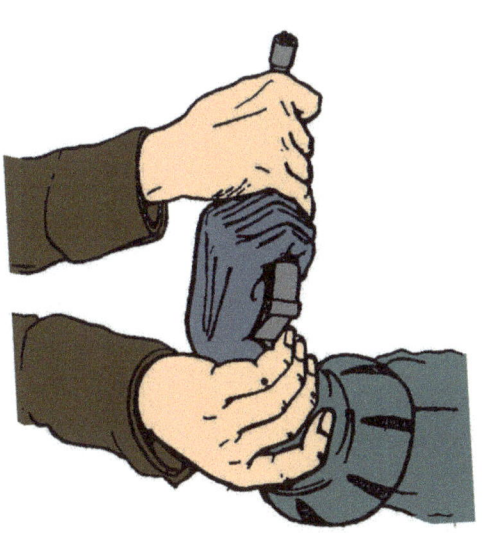

Fig. 129

Fig. 130

NO. 30—DISARMING AN OPPONENT OF HIS PISTOL (cont.)

C—Disarming from Behind

1. Hold your arms as in Fig. 131.
2. Turn rapidly inwards towards your left-hand side, passing your left arm over and around your opponent's right forearm, as near the wrist as possible, and bring your left hand up your chest (Fig. 132).

Note.—It is impossible for him to shoot you or release his arm from this grip.

3. Immediately the arm is locked, knee him in the testicles with your right knee and chin-jab him with your right hand, as in Fig. 133.

Note.—If the knee blow and chin jab do not make him release his hold of the pistol, go after his eyes with the fingers of your right hand.

Fig. 131

Fig. 132

Fig. 133

NO. 30—DISARMING AN OPPONENT OF HIS PISTOL (cont.)

D—Disarming from behind (Alternative Method)

The difference between this method and that shown on the previous page is that the initial attack is made with your right arm instead of your left.

1. Hold your arms as in Fig. 134.
2. Turn rapidly outwards towards your right-hand side, passing your right arm over and around your opponent's right forearm, as near the wrist as possible, and bring your right hand up your chest (Fig. 135).

Note.—As in the previous method, it is impossible for him to shoot you or release his arm from this grip.

3. Immediately the arm is locked, strike your opponent across the throat, as near the "Adam's apple" as possible, with an edge-of-the-hand blow of your left hand, as in Fig. 136.

Note.—Should your opponent not release his hold of the pistol, follow up by pressing with your right leg on the outside of his right leg, as in Fig. 137, and break his leg.

Fig. 134   Fig. 135

Fig. 136   Fig. 137

NO. 30—DISARMING AN OPPONENT OF HIS PISTOL (concl.)

E—Disarming a Third Party

It is quite possible that, upon coming around a corner, you find one of your own men being held up, as in Fig. 138.

1. Come up on your opponent's pistol arm, seize his pistol and hand from underneath, simultaneously coming down hard with your left hand on his arm, just above the elbow joint (Fig. 139).
2. Jerk his hand upwards and backwards, and force his elbow upwards with your left hand, at the same time pivoting inwards on your left foot. Continue the pressure of your right hand in a downward direction (Fig. 140).

Note A.—This will cause him to release his hold of the pistol; if necessary, knee him in the testicles with your right knee.

Note B.—The initial upward movement of the pistol (¶ 2) is recommended in preference to a downward blow because the pistol is jerked away from the direction of your own man very quickly, and it also permits you to obtain a hold of his pistol hand, from which you can force him to release his hold of the weapon. Further, your own man can, by means of a kick to the opponent's testicles, considerably help you in disarming.

Fig. 138   Fig. 139

Fig. 140

(8)

www.ingramcontent.com/pod-product-compliance
Lightning Source LLC
Chambersburg PA
CBHW061252230426
43664CB00025B/2935